ANIMALS HEAD TO HEAD

Alligator
VS.
Crocodile

This book is dedicated to the memory of Lucy Owen,
who really cared about this series.

ISABEL THOMAS

Raintree

CHICAGO, ILLINOIS

For information, address the publisher:
Raintree, 100 N. LaSalle, Suite 1200
Chicago, IL 60602
Customer Service   888–363–4266
Visit our website at www.raintreelibrary.com

Editorial: Dan Nunn and Katie Shepherd
Design: Victoria Bevan
and Bridge Creative Services Ltd
Picture Research: Hannah Taylor
and Rebecca Sodergren
Production: Duncan Gilbert

Originated by Chroma Graphics Pte. Ltd
Printed and bound in China by
South China Printing Company

The paper used to print this book comes from
sustainable resources.

10 09 08 07 06
10 9 8 7 6 5 4 3 2 1

**Library of Congress Cataloging-in-Publiation
Data**
Thomas, Isabel, 1980-
  Alligator vs. crocodile / Isabel Thomas.
    p. cm. -- (Animals head to head)
  Includes bibliographical references (p.   ) and index.
  ISBN-13: 978-1-4109-2395-0 (lib. bdg.)
  ISBN-10: 1-4109-2395-9 (lib. bdg.)
  ISBN-13: 978-1-4109-2402-5 (pbk.)
  ISBN-10: 1-4109-2402-5 (pbk.)
  1. American alligator--Juvenile literature. 2.
Crocodylus porosus--Juvenile literature. I. Title:
Alligator versus crocodile. II. Title. III. Series:
 Thomas, Isabel, 1980-   Animals head to head.
QL666.C925T48 2006
597.98'4--dc22
                          2005035015

Acknowledgments
The publishers would like to thank the following for
permission to reproduce photographs:

ANTPhoto.com p. **24** (Mick Davey); Ardea p. **17**
(Cancalosi); Corbis pp. **16** (Paul A. Souders), **18**
(David A. Northcott), **19** (Ron Sanford), **26 left**
(W. Perry Conway), **28** (Davis Factor); DK Images
p. **7**; FLPA pp. **8** (Foto Natura/Martin Woike), **25**
(Gerard Lacz), **26 right** (Minden Pictures/Cyril
Ruoso); Getty Images pp. **11** (Science Faction), **20**
(The Image Bank); Naturepl.com pp. **4 right** (Peter
Scoones), **12** (Jeff Rotman), **13** (Peter Scoones), **15**
(Nigel Marven), **29** (Jeff Foott); NHPA pp. **4 left**
(ANT Photo Library), **6** (Patrick Fagot), **21** (Jonathan
& Angela Scott), **22** (Jonathan & Angela Scott);
Photolibrary.com pp. **9**, **10** (Philippe Henry),
14 (Index Stock Imagery).

Cover photograph of an alligator reproduced
with permission of Ardea/M. Watson. Cover
photograph of a crocodile reproduced with
permission of Corbis/Martin Harvey.

Every effort has been made to contact copyright
holders of any material reproduced in this book.
Any omissions will be rectified in subsequent
printings if notice is given to the publishers.

Disclaimer
All the Internet addresses (URLs) given in this book
were valid at the time of going to press. However,
due to the dynamic nature of the Internet, some
addresses may have changed, or sites may have
changed or ceased to exist since publication. While
the author and publishers regret any inconvenience
this may cause readers, no responsibility for any
such changes can be accepted by either the author
or the publishers.

Contents

Any words appearing in the text in bold, **like this**, are explained in the glossary.

Meet the Reptiles

It's dusk, and thirsty animals need their last drink of the day. But on both sides of the planet, hidden dangers lurk in the water. In the rivers of northern Australia and the swamps of Florida, two of the world's biggest **reptiles** lie in wait for their dinner.

Crocodiles and alligators are both **predators**. They survive by hunting and eating other animals. Every part of a predator's body is perfectly designed to help it find, catch, and eat meat.

Around the world, crocodiles kill up to 1,500 people every year.

In the last 60 years, American alligators have killed only 18 people.

4

Danger in the water

The biggest alligators in the world are American alligators. They live in the marshes and swamplands of the southern United States. The largest crocodiles are found in Asia as well as the Australia and New Zealand area. They are called saltwater crocodiles because they can survive in both freshwater and seawater.

American alligators and saltwater crocodiles are known as deadly hunters. But which reptile is the champion predator?

This map shows where American alligators and saltwater crocs live in the wild.

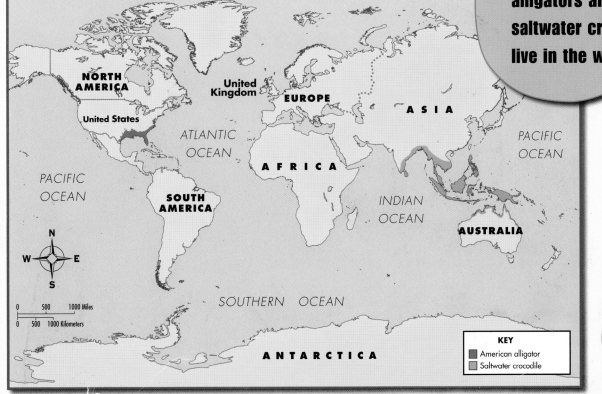

Size and Strength

The biggest **predators** have the best choice of food. Male crocodiles and alligators use their size and strength to catch large **prey**. Size is also important for attracting females. Only the largest and fiercest males get to **breed**.

On and on and on

The longest American alligator ever found is reported to have measured more than 18 feet (5.6 meters) from **snout** to tail. Most males grow to nearly 15 feet (about 4.5 meters). Saltwater crocodiles are even bigger—up to 23 feet (7 meters) long!

23 ft. (7 m)

A male saltwater crocodile can weigh as much as fifteen men.

Powerful predators

A strong body helps an animal scare off predators. It also helps it become a better predator itself.

Saltwater crocodiles are some of the toughest animals in the world. They can overpower almost anything, including buffalo, cattle, horses, monkeys, and even sharks!

The American alligator is the largest type of alligator in the world.

15 ft. (4.5 m)

Snout power

Heavy **snouts** and strong necks help crocodiles and alligators drag large **prey** into water. Then they hold their victim down until it drowns. Sometimes they smash their head against a victim's legs to knock it over.

Alligators may be shorter than crocodiles, but they have larger heads. Its heavy head helps an alligator force its way through bushy plants in the American marshes and swamplands.

Heavy snouts help alligators grip prey tightly in a struggle.

Body armor

Like all **reptiles**, crocodiles and alligators have scaly skin. Some of their scales are extra tough with thick, bony plates. This **armor** protects the **predators** when they are wrestling their prey. Leathery skin also keeps crocodiles and alligators from getting sunburned!

Saltwater crocodiles have thinner skin over their necks. This makes it easier to turn and twist away from enemies. But it also means they have a weak spot.

Tough scales protect a crocodile from the hooves and claws of struggling prey.

WINNER

HEAD TO HEAD

	Croc	Gator	
Size	10	7	Gator fails to measure up.
Strength	9	10	Gator head-butts his way ahead!

Speed and Endurance

Alligators and crocodiles have bodies designed for both land and water.

On land, crocs and gators usually move very slowly. The bigger they are, the harder it gets to move quickly. Their heavy bodies and short legs make them look clumsy. Long fat tails drag along the ground. They can only run for a short distance, so humans and other animals are safe if they stay a few yards away. But in water, crocs and gators are fantastic swimmers and **agile** hunters!

Crocs and gators can walk, run, or crawl on land.

Swimming

Gators and crocs usually swim slowly. They hardly make the water ripple. Saltwater crocodiles are the best at swimming long distances. They have been spotted far out at sea, hundreds of miles from land. Sometimes they drift to save energy.

Crocs at sea
Saltwater crocodiles can stay in the sea for several weeks. Alligators need to stay near fresh water.

When crocs and gators swim, their muscle-packed tails move from side to side, pushing them through the water.

Legs fold in to make bodies more **streamlined** as they cruise along.

Webbed feet help with steering, braking, and balance.

11

Ambush!

Crocodiles and alligators spend hours resting in the sun or floating in the water without moving. But when there is a chance to catch **prey**, these big **reptiles** explode into action!

Gators and crocs prefer to attack from the water. They flick their powerful tail for a burst of speed. Sometimes they leave the water and crawl a few yards up the bank at up to 11 mph (18 kph). Their prey is taken by surprise.

Tired out

Crocs and gators get very tired after hunting. They take a long time to recover, moving slowly to save energy.

A crocodile's tail is strong enough to launch it straight up into the air!

Endurance

No reptile can breathe underwater, but crocodiles and alligators are good at holding their breath. This makes it easy for them to hold prey underwater until it drowns.

Temperature control

Unlike **mammals**, reptiles cannot produce their own body heat. If they want to warm up, they have to sit in the sun. When they get too hot, they plunge into water.

American alligators have an extra challenge. The southern United States can get cold in winter. To keep warm, alligators shelter in burrows or pools of warm water called gator holes.

Alligators are expert divers. They can stay underwater for over two hours!

HEAD TO HEAD

	Croc	Gator	
Speed	7	5	Croc leaves gator standing on the beach.
Endurance	7	9	Don't hold your breath croc, you'll never beat gator!

13

A Surprise Attack

Crocodiles and alligators have **senses** designed for hunting. An excellent sense of smell tells them if an animal is friend or food. Great eyesight helps them figure out if a victim is close enough to grab. Special clear eyelids allow them to hunt underwater.

What was that?

Crocs and gators can hear even the quietest sounds. A crocodile can hear its babies squawk while they are still inside the **eggs**! The noise tells the adult that the young crocs are ready to hatch.

Special slit-like pupils open wide, so a croc or gator can see well in low light.

pupil

14

Super sense

On a starless and moonless night, even crocs and gators cannot see much. But they can still attack with deadly precision. Tiny **pressure detectors** cover their head and jaws. These small gray spots help the **reptiles** feel the tiniest ripple in the water.

Saltwater crocodiles have these pressure detectors all over their body. When something moves nearby, the croc knows exactly where to aim his jaws. Anything that disturbs the water is in danger!

The small dot on each scale is a tiny pressure detector.

Saving energy

Most **predators** use amazing skills of **stealth** to catch **prey**. Crocodiles and alligators can only move quickly for a few seconds, so they need to be as close as possible before attacking.

Instead of swimming around looking for prey, they float in the same spot and wait for their next meal to come to them! This saves all their energy for the attack.

This croc's bumpy brown skin makes him look like a floating log.

Unseen danger

Crocs and gators are almost invisible as they lie waiting for a victim. Only the eyes, ears, and tip of the nose float above the surface. They can hear, see, and smell without being detected.

As soon as an animal or bird gets close enough, the **reptile** launches a violent attack. By the time the prey sees the croc or gator it is usually too late!

Dark green skin blends in with the gator's watery habitat to provide camouflage.

WINNER

	Croc	Gator	
HEAD TO HEAD			
Senses	10	8	Croc feels his way to victory.
Camouflage	10	10	Both are hard to spot.

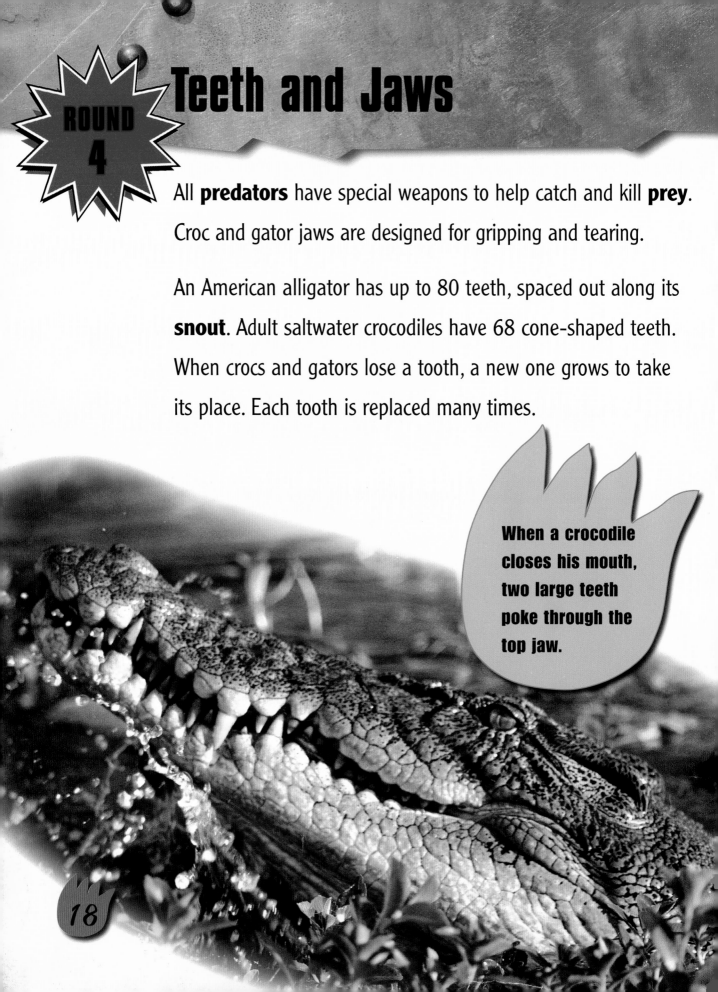

Teeth and Jaws

All **predators** have special weapons to help catch and kill **prey**. Croc and gator jaws are designed for gripping and tearing.

An American alligator has up to 80 teeth, spaced out along its **snout**. Adult saltwater crocodiles have 68 cone-shaped teeth. When crocs and gators lose a tooth, a new one grows to take its place. Each tooth is replaced many times.

When a crocodile closes his mouth, two large teeth poke through the top jaw.

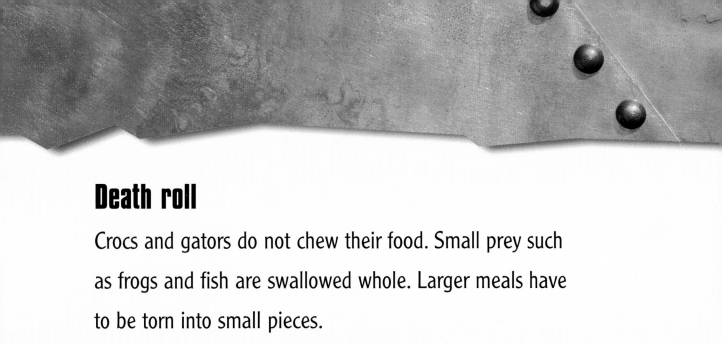

Death roll

Crocs and gators do not chew their food. Small prey such as frogs and fish are swallowed whole. Larger meals have to be torn into small pieces.

Crocs and gators use a terrifying "death roll" to tear up food. They grab the prey in their powerful jaws and spin around in the water. When they have removed a chunk of meat, they tip their head back and swallow it in one gulp.

An alligator can chomp his way through more than 2,000 teeth in a lifetime!

Jaw power

A huge skull and massive jaw muscles turn croc and gator teeth into deadly weapons. In the 1970s, an Australian saltwater crocodile became famous for attacking motorboats. He destroyed more than 20 engines with his powerful jaws.

But the strongest jaws in the world belong to American alligators. It would be easier to lift a car than to force an alligator's jaws open!

A powerful grip stops slippery prey from escaping.

Nothing goes to waste

Crocs and gators eat every part of their **prey**. Their stomach acid can even dissolve bones and feathers. They often swallow stones to help them grind up hard foods like turtle shells.

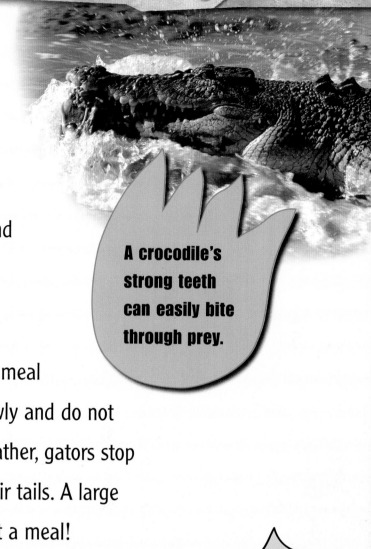

A crocodile's strong teeth can easily bite through prey.

No appetite

Crocs and gators only need about one meal a week. This is because they move slowly and do not make their own body heat. In cold weather, gators stop eating and live on the fat stored in their tails. A large gator can survive for two years without a meal!

WINNER

HEAD TO HEAD

	Croc	Gator	
Teeth	7	8	Gator wins with a toothy grin.
Jaws	9	10	It's a crushing defeat for croc!

21

Hunting and Fighting Skills

We have seen what makes crocodiles and alligators such fearsome **predators**.

They hunt by surprising their victims. Floating silently in shallow water, crocs and gators can see, smell, hear, or feel anything that comes close. With perfect timing, they explode out of the water and grab the **prey**.

Small animals are killed with a single crushing bite. Larger prey is dragged into the water to be drowned. Nothing is safe— some crocs will even eat their own brothers and sisters!

Crocodiles will eat almost anything that comes close enough.

Thinking ahead

Crocs and gators can be clever. They learn when animals come to drink. Then they wait patiently to attack.

Gators and crocs begin hunting when they are very young. They start with small prey such as dragonflies and snails. Even tiny crocs know that they have to stay hidden until their victims come close.

Top predators

Alligators and crocodiles are the top predators in their **habitat**. Few animals would dare try to eat an adult gator or croc!

A food chain shows what eats what in a habitat.

Grass grows alongside swamps.

Calves eat grass.

Alligators eat calves.

23

Fights with other males involve hissing, head bashing, and biting.

Killer crocs
Gators often run away if they are losing a battle. But young crocs sometimes fight to the death.

Fighting fit

Crocs and gators are brilliant fighters. Sharp **senses** make it hard for other animals to sneak up on them. **Armored** bodies and strong jaws are deadly weapons.

Fight for the right to mate

Male gators and crocs that want to attract females will wrestle any males that invade their **territory**. The biggest males show off their strength by swimming close to the surface of the water. They slap their heads onto the water and thrash their tails.

Crocs also attack animals that try to eat their babies. **Predators** such as lizards, baboons, and other crocodiles all like the taste of **reptile eggs**.

But strangely, crocs and gators do not fight over food. If a crocodile catches a large water buffalo, other crocodiles will often come and share it. They take turns eating.

Fighting is risky for alligators. They might lose a leg or part of their tail.

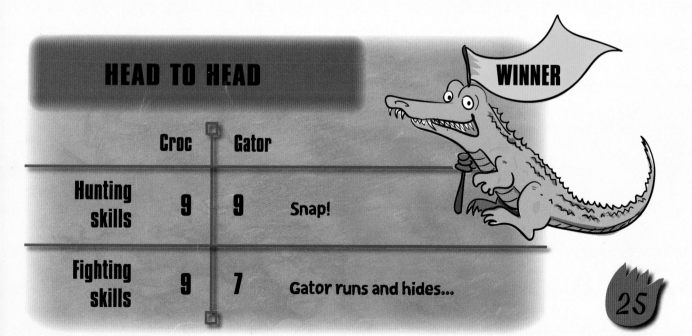

HEAD TO HEAD

	Croc	Gator	
Hunting skills	9	9	Snap!
Fighting skills	9	7	Gator runs and hides...

WINNER

Who Wins?

Deadly **stealth**, bone-crunching jaws, and **armored** skin make both crocodiles and alligators fantastic **predators**.

But which predator is the best? American alligators and saltwater crocodiles would never meet in the wild. But what might happen if they did?

Reptile rage

No male croc or gator likes to find another male in his **territory**. First they might try to warn each other off by hissing and showing their teeth. Each one would puff out his chest and raise his tail to make himself look bigger.

Then they would bash their heads together in a test of strength. Crushing bites would be aimed at legs and tails.

These huge **reptiles** would be very well matched. American alligators have bigger heads and the most powerful jaws in the world. But saltwater crocodiles grow up to 6.5 feet (2 meters) longer and are strong enough to swim across oceans. They have been known to hunt leopards and sharks, and attack humans without being provoked!

Faced with this ferocious giant, the alligator would run away first.

HEAD TO HEAD

	Croc	Gator
Size	10	7
Strength	9	10
Speed	7	5
Endurance	7	9
Senses	10	8
Camouflage	10	10
Teeth	7	8
Jaws	9	10
Hunting skills	9	9
Fighting skills	9	7
Total	87/100	83/100

Cunning croc wins the crown!

27

The Real Fight

American alligators and saltwater crocodiles are not likely to meet in the wild. But they have a much worse enemy—humans.

Like **reptiles**, people like to live near water. They use up space and catch the food that crocs and gators eat. They kill reptiles for meat and skins, or because they are afraid. They **pollute** the water with poisonous **chemicals**.

Killed for fashion

For more than 100 years, crocodiles and alligators have been killed for their skins. By 1970, all crocodiles and alligators were **endangered**.

Thousands of croc and gator skins are traded around the world each year.

Changing times
If you looked for a crocodile book in the 1920s, you would have found one called *A Few Hints on Crocodile Shooting*!

A double threat

Hunting alligators and crocodiles is now illegal in most countries. More than one million American alligators and 300,000 saltwater crocodiles now live in the wild. But other types of crocodile and alligator are still in great danger from **poachers**. Even worse, their **habitats** are being destroyed.

People still buy crocodile and alligator skins, but most now come from animals raised on ranches or farms. The farms will help prevent crocodiles and alligators from becoming **extinct**. But these champion predators will only survive in the wild if their habitats are protected as well.

Raising crocodiles and alligators on farms means that fewer are taken from the wild.

Glossary

agile combination of speed and skill when moving

armor protective layer covering an animal

breed to have babies

camouflage body features that allow animals to blend into their habitat, to avoid being seen by predators or prey

chemicals any materials used in, or made by, science and industry

egg large cell with a protective covering, inside which baby reptiles grow

endangered in danger of dying out completely

endurance strength and energy to survive in difficult conditions

extinct when a type of animal no longer exists

fresh water water that is not salty, such as the water in rivers and lakes

habitat place where an animal lives

mammal animals that can make their own body heat and produce milk for their babies

poacher person who hunts or fishes animals when it is against the law

pollute to damage air, land, or water

predator animal that hunts, kills, and eats other animals

pressure detector part of the body that can sense when things push against it

prey animal that is caught, killed, and eaten by another animal as food

reptile animal that can't make its own body heat and has scales

senses ways in which an animal gets information about its surroundings

snout part of an animal's head that juts forward, containing the nose and mouth

stealth doing something slowly and quietly to avoid being noticed

streamlined smooth object that allows water to flow over it easily

territory area that an animal lives in and defends against rivals

30

More Information

Books

Pyers, Greg. *Why Am I a Reptile?* Chicago: Raintree, 2006.
Read this book to learn more about the biology of crocodiles and alligators.

Solway, Andrew. *Wild Predators: Deadly Reptiles.* Chicago: Heinemann Library, 2005.
This book explores the lives of the most dangerous reptiles, including crocodiles and alligators.

Spilsbury, Richard, and Louise Spilsbury. *Animals Under Threat: Alligator.* Chicago: Heinemann Library, 2004.
This book focuses on the threats alligators face from humans.

Websites

www.nwf.org—visit this site and search for "crocodile" or "alligator" to find photos, articles, and facts.

www.seaworld.org—visit this site and click on "animal info" to find information on alligators and crocodiles, including physical traits and fun facts.

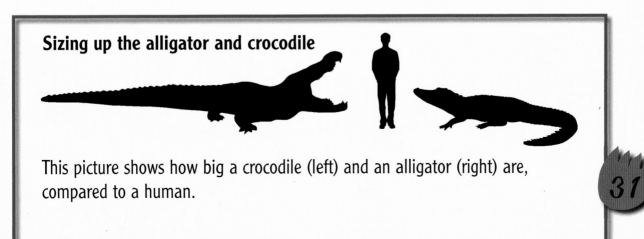

Sizing up the alligator and crocodile

This picture shows how big a crocodile (left) and an alligator (right) are, compared to a human.

Index